BROKEN PLACES

The world breaks everyone, and afterward,
some are strong at the broken places.
~ Ernest Hemingway

by RACHEL THOMPSON

Booktrope Editions
Seattle WA 2014

Cover Design by Shari Ryan

Edited by Mary Ward Menke

Print ISBN 978-1-62015-689-6

EPUB ISBN 978-1-62015-700-8

Library of Congress Control Number: 2014922627

TABLE OF CONTENTS

ACKNOWLEDGMENTS

This is my fourth book (is that possible? Wow!), and this time, acknowledgments are easy.

Thank you to my family and friends, as always. I fold you up and hold you in my heart, especially my folks. Many survivors are estranged from their parents and I'm blessed to not only have their support, but also encouragement in sharing my story.

To Booktrope for believing in my words; Katherine Sears, Jessica Swift, Bobbi, Mary, Stephanie Konat, Justin Bog, Shari Ryan, and Bennet Pomerantz for your insights; Kate and Naomi for your invaluable help.

And most of all, thank you to my street team, fans and supporters, but most especially, to all the survivors. Your brave voices make a difference.

FOREWORD

Rachel Thompson is ground zero for one of the most powerful healing movements for survivors of childhood sexual abuse that I, as a mental health professional, have ever seen. She will never tell you this herself. She's too humble to do so. But I'll tell you because knowing the breadth of Rachel's heart and the depth of her compassion for fellow survivors will help you understand not only why she's written this book but why it is so powerful and healing.

Rachel and I are both survivors of childhood sexual abuse. We are very familiar with the corrosive burden of shame that abuse heaps on survivors at an age when no one should be expected to carry anything heavier than a book bag. But there she stood, not even an adolescent, facing the shame of the abuse, testifying in two trials against her abuser and then having to face his whole family every day as she walked past their house and his children at school.

Like many survivors she learned to fly under the radar to avoid the eyes that bore into her, knowing both her greatest secret and her greatest horror. She learned to hide anything that could be construed as a flaw and began expecting and exhibiting and striving for nothing less than perfection from herself. If she were perfect, she believed, her shame would become invisible to others. She mastered the art of calling no attention to herself unless her performance and achievement were stellar.

She carried that skill into adulthood, becoming an expert in her chosen career, while making her way through life in those arenas where the shame of her abuse made her feel "less than." As survivors, we are keenly aware of those parts of ourselves that we believe were damaged during our abuse. We live in fear of those shortcomings being exposed, our secrets spilling out in front of the entire world. This terrifies us. To protect ourselves we dash from shrub to wall to tree in life's landscape. We constantly look ahead of us for the next place to hide. Then we scuttle, as quickly and as quietly as we can, to that sanctuary. Exposure is excruciating because it allows shame to catch up with us. And when it does it is a merciless beast, hollowing us out with its acidic attack. At the very core of ourselves we harbor our greatest fear—that shame will leave us so empty that our fragile shell crumbles and blows away.

The only way to rid ourselves of shame is to name it and speak of it. In her book *Daring Greatly*, Brené Brown writes, "Shame derives its power from being unspeakable…Shame hates having words wrapped around it. If we speak shame, it begins to wither. Just as the way exposure to light was deadly for gremlins, language and story bring light to shame and destroy it." (Brown, B. [2012] Daring Greatly. New York: NY. Gotham) Naming our shame is hard enough; speaking of it is terrifying.

But, in December of 2012 Rachel sloughed off her silence on the issue and published her compilation of essays and poems that tell of her experience of childhood sexual abuse in her book *Broken Pieces*. She did the one thing every survivor fears the most. And she did it with so much raw truth and eloquence that *Broken Pieces* became a best seller. More than its commercial success, though, is the larger purpose the book serves— it gives voice and courage to other survivors who see themselves in Rachel's words.

From the seemingly simple, yet enormously frightening task of speaking her truth, Rachel continued to shed her shame and speak out as an advocate for other survivors. In early 2013 she started an online support group for survivors of childhood sexual abuse. This group has become a powerful healing force in the lives of its members, as it gives them a safe place to find their voice and share their truth.

In January 2014, Rachel started a Twitter chat for survivors, #SexAbuseChat. I have been lucky enough to co-host this chat with her. It's given me a front seat view of the community of people who gather every Tuesday night to provide one another with support, encouragement, and validation. Through the support group and Twitter chat, I've seen more healing taking place than I have in the seventeen years that I've been a therapist. Creating community allows many survivors to be healed at the same time, which can sometimes be just as powerful as working one-on-one in my counseling practice.

This is the power of one survivor breaking through the curtain of invisibility and in turn, providing a safe place for other survivors to do so as well. This is the power of Rachel Thompson stepping out in tremendous courage, starting an avalanche of healing that has already touched thousands and will continue to sweep outward touching many, many more. This is just the beginning.

With her new book, *Broken Places*, Rachel continues her brave work. As she shares in this volume of her work I want you to know how amazing it is that she is even speaking up. She has sacrificed her own invisibility to speak her truth so the echoes can spread out, reaching those who need to know there is life beyond the place where they are crouching down, hiding.

If you are a survivor of childhood sexual abuse I encourage you to read Rachel's words knowing that she understands where you are and what you have been through. Draw courage from her story and reach out. Rachel is readily available on social media. She will embrace you wholeheartedly and invite you to join in on the many projects we have undertaken to help survivors heal. You don't have to be ready to speak up and share your story. You just have to reach out. Because Rachel told her story—and continues to share her experiences and how they shaped her—many, many others are finding the courage to tell theirs. And when the time is right for those who choose to end their silence, Rachel will be there to listen.

Bobbi Parish
Author, Survivor, Therapist and
Trauma Recovery Coach

About Bobbi Parish

Bobbi is a therapist and trauma recovery coach who works with adult survivors of childhood abuse. Herself a survivor of childhood abuse, she uses her experience and expertise to co-host both #SexAbuseChat on Twitter and a weekly Google hangout for survivors. As a co-founder of the #NoMoreShame Project she works to provide education, support and coaching to trauma survivors as well as a platform for them to publish their stories, poetry and memoirs. Bobbi is also an author with one published book, *Create Your Personal Sacred Text*, and has two others in the works. She is a single mother from the Pacific Northwest currently sequestered to the state of Texas. Sparkly shoes are her personal kryptonite. You can learn more about Bobbi at BobbiParish.com and NoMoreShameProject.com.

TRIGGER WARNING

This book contains essays and poetry on sexual abuse, emotions, love, and loss. Some subject matter, while not explicit, could potentially trigger survivors or individuals bothered by sensitive material. Discretion is advised.

INTRODUCTION

*We feel that to reveal embarrassing or private things, we have given
someone something, that, like a primitive person fearing that a
photographer will steal his soul, we identify our secrets, our past and
their blotches, with our identity, that revealing our habits or losses or
deeds somehow makes one less of oneself.*

~ Dave Eggers, *A Heartbreaking Work of Staggering Genius*

WOMEN TRAVEL TO MANY PLACES in our minds, particularly
when in pain.

Sometimes we're holding on to the fringes of our sanity by
remembering the taste of lemon frosting spread across a tentative
finger. The problem with the memory of something so deliciously
sweet is that our craving for it becomes uncontrollable.

MIND

Cravings are funny things. Ask any pregnant woman. We wake
up knowing that if we don't have that chocolate donut right now,

heads will roll. We can't explain it; we don't understand it ourselves. We only know that something triggered us to need that taste, and only that taste, or life as we know it, and those around us, will end.

And that's not women being dramatic—that's us, being women. Senses engaged, the ghost of the taste moving us—circling, waiting with a driving, icy wind, propelling us to find that one exact flavor in order for it to finally leave us in peace.

The sugary licks may not be good for us, but still we search inside our books and letters, looking for the words that can satisfy, knowing it will never come.

Maybe tomorrow.

BODY

Behavior is a funny thing—our bodies and senses revealing that which we doubtfully understand or even acknowledge. We may know we are moving forward with something we can't quite pin down, only know that a part of us needs it. Sometimes that's enough.

That is rarely enough for those around us, our lovers and families, to understand. Loving and lying often go hand in hand, not to hurt, but to not hurt.

No one is immune. We are human. Our minds drive our actions, but we detach in order to make it through. No matter what you know, unconscious habit derived from our past drives us. It's why we eventually wake up, searching, always searching, knowing change is coming, carrying pieces forward.

Into tomorrow.

SOUL

We know what it's like for our soul to burn with longing, an ache so great we thank ephemeral spirits for reminding us that love exists. Is that what drives us? Men longing for the touch of the woman they love, but make do with the touch of any woman who will quench their own craving.

Women hiding in another's love, away from the demands of the man they once burned for, one who no longer drenches their souls in the drumming of all-consuming need.

We move, we grow, we need for something we hear calling to us in the mist. Risk implied, nothing guaranteed when it comes to feeding our souls, except finding it ourselves.

We are alone in our search for peace or love or contentment. We move, we dance, we love, deciding how to pull it all together with a combination of instinct, desire, and hope.

Until tomorrow.

MIND

KINDRED

Happiness is hard to recognize because it leaves no scars. Pain leaves evidence — we know where we've been.

WE GO ABOUT OUR DAYS JUST LIKE YOU. We are survivors, you see, not monsters. We don't wear a banner of yellow police tape across our foreheads that screams "victim." You wouldn't know us as you walk on the street or see us sipping hot beverages in the coffee shop.

As we walk by you, we subconsciously size you up. Are you a threat? Are you judging us in some way? Would you understand? We look at your eyes. The eyes carry the wounds. The eyes know damage. Damaged people recognize other damaged people, and we let you in.

We are kindred.

This Mind section talks about the subconscious way our mind works, the damage we don't even know has been done. I lived for years, decades really, not knowing or understanding the effects that the childhood sexual abuse had on me. I thought, like many others, that it happened, it was in the past, move on. Keep the past in the past.

Except, as Einstein stated so eloquently, "the separation between past, present, and future is only an illusion." This explains why the mind throws flashbacks at us—like a toddler wanting attention right then and there, the mind doesn't care, or has no concept, about time.

Our brains protect us and fool us. Learning to trust ourselves is a constant balancing act. Here is mine.

SILENCE

HIS HANDS WERE ROUGH, the hands of a working man. As he slides closer on the seat, his large legs pushed mine down, making them useless for running away.

He knew what he was doing.

A father. Of girls. Girls my age. Did he touch them this same way, I couldn't help but wonder, in a foreign way my own father would never, and had never, touched me? This isn't how it was supposed to work, was it? He was not speaking my language.

My eleven-year-old mind didn't grasp exactly what he wanted — this was my neighbor, a middle-aged military man, one hand searching for my non-existent breasts, his fingers working their way into my shorts.

I froze. This wasn't happening.

In a silent scream, I flew away, watching from the old oak tree that spread its arms the length of several men — wise, knowing branches holding the memories of other little girls. I held their tiny hands as we waited for him to be done, ghosts of innocence clinging to the bark, not even the rain able to wash away his dirty, prying fingers.

Taking my shaking silence as permission, he continued with his exploration. As my quiet tears spilled, I watched from my safe little tree perch, knowing somehow that even though he'd stop at some point, nothing would ever look the same.

Finding the courage in my ability to fly, I spoke: "please, stop." When he pulled out his gun weighted with a meaning I couldn't quite comprehend, placing it silently in my hand, I understood that my words didn't matter to a man intent on speaking the language of the unforgiven. I waited patiently on my sturdy oak, holding onto the wispy ghosts for strength until he…finished.

Making it clear that my family was in danger, that dark gun laden with a threat I could only imagine in my worst middle-of-the-night nightmares, enough to buy my silence. No quiet murmurings, only a binding secret replacing my innocence with shame.

Children inherently understand the art of negotiation. Even I knew that this was definitely not a fair trade. I never agreed to the terms of the deal, only to a heavy silence I didn't know how to carry.

My world of laughter and dolls and joy didn't end that day, but it changed—I now carried a burden that didn't allow me to speak, that hid inside me, weaving its way deeper to a place that expanded and contracted with every breath, that reminded me only in hushed whispers, "Don't tell."

SHAME

SHAME DOESN'T LIKE TO TALK. She prefers to walk through a room, the center of attention, the girl that all the boys dream of, all eyes on her, flash and heels and lips and eyes, and hair.

Shame is the one everyone talks about but nobody talks to.

Shame wears pretty, tiny bits of clothes, fancy makeup, and drives a cool, red, fast car, the kind all little girls dream of when they play with their Barbies. She has all the hottest boyfriends, and even the occasional hot girlfriend, who shows up late to the cool kids' parties as if she's too good to be there anyway, and besides, "this place blows," she tells her jock hottie of the day as she sashays her tiny hips poured into her "$1200-a-pop-paid-for-by-daddy" jeans out the door to the next coke-fueled gig.

Shame has a secret. Shame saturates herself with distractions, partying all day and all night because she's desperately sad, filled with the loneliness of the lost, her heart a shell scraped so deep because she left it in an alley one night with her pride and her virginity when one large man pinched and shoved and filled and grabbed in ways she cringes to remember, in tears and rages, in nightmares and flashes she can't ever discuss with another human.

Because he was an animal and that makes her one, too.

Shame carries this animal in her skin, unable to shake his eyes boring into hers as she fought and kicked while he held her down, sticking his furious cock into her. As she watched from above, she wondered aloud why he even need to bother with a live girl; if all he wanted was a hole, he could have just as easily found some sort of household appliance to stick it in. A hole was a hole was a hole.

But he didn't hear her mumbled words.

Nobody hears Shame. They follow her, watching her every move, but they don't see her. They don't see her terror, how she shakes alone in her room at night, how she wakes up covered in the slimy sweat of the animal, smelling his stink, flashing on his fetid breath, his flaccid penis finally moving away from her face, forever wiping his semen from her lips in the hour-long, skin-burning hot showers she takes

every night,

every night,

every night

scrubbing away that which will never fucking die.

Nobody talks to Shame. They look at her, they stare at her, but they don't embrace her. She's this creature, this thing nobody will ever love or soothe, or even acknowledge. Shame knows this.

She was born out of fear and terror and hurt. She knows that she is nobody's friend.

Because, after all, who wants to be friends with Shame?

MINIMIZATION AND DENIAL

PART OF MY PAST with the neighbor is crystal clear—watching him from the pool with what was clearly an erection, not understanding why he had this *thing* in his shorts (I had a very private father and no brothers, so that equipment was completely foreign to me), the girls braiding each other's hair as we waited patiently in line in the hot summer sun for our ride on his scooter, never wondering why some took longer than others. It wasn't for us to say, was it? We were only children.

Other parts are fuzzier—now, forty years later, I have waves of clarity and waves of gray. There was kissing, inappropriate touching, no penetration. Anything beyond that is a blur, which is perhaps a blessing.

But what's loud and clear is this: my folks telling people who found out about it that what happened to me "wasn't as bad" as what happened to the other, younger girls. So I grew up thinking well, fine then. It was disgusting, wrong, and gross, but my parents say I'm fine, so I must be fine.

(It's worth noting that I don't blame them—they didn't understand or know how to deal with this situation. As my mom says, "We were stupid. We just didn't know what to do.")

But I wasn't fine. I didn't understand that the rushes of panic I would have when faced with a troublesome situation could be directly tied to those same feelings of fear when I was abused. I didn't understand that the chemical structure of the brain actually changes in response to terror and fear. I didn't know that the nightmares I still have to this day are correlated to that time, and would be referred to as PTSD.

For any survivor, these types of stressors are known as "triggers." It wasn't until my late thirties that I sought therapy, unlocking much of what I had carried for so very long. Decades later I still can't get my mind around it all because there's just so much we don't know about the brain. Understanding triggers is a daily lesson for me.

And it's okay. I love, I breathe, I work, I write, I live. What happened does not stop me.

Strong and responsible, that's me—your typical Capricorn. I get the job done, and my ambition drives me in a way that rarely lets up. Not a victim, never a victim. Only a survivor.

Still, the shame that survivors carry can be an incredibly heavy burden—though we know and understand that rationally, what happened was not our fault, and therefore, no shame should be attached...it is.

It always, always is.

Because no matter how much we've come to terms with our abuse—no matter the severity—the fact that someone invaded us when we were children is always there. Minimization and denial are common and frankly, understandable in abuse situations—few of us can really understand how it even happens, especially to little children. Guilt, shame and total abhorrence are normal reactions.

I can't imagine the guilt my parents felt and perhaps still feel. It wasn't their fault, though. It certainly wasn't mine. It was HIS.

The person I was then, the child full of innocence and wonder at the world, she ceased to exist after only eleven years. Those kisses he stole were oh so much more—he took pieces of my soul, from places I will never recover.

In a way, he did me a favor. He showed me that people can be bad. They can wear a suit of goodness, writhing with snakes underneath, coiled and waiting for that one singular moment to strike. When they have you alone, for nobody can see. That people are rarely, if ever, what they first seem.

Innocence lost.

Strength found.

SHAME IN SILENCE

Shame pulls the cover of shadow around her,
burying herself in the smoky silence

Safe in pretending
she dons her blinding mask

What is right, what should be, makes her cry,
but Confusion holds her hand

Shame befriends Fear,
Fear befriends Silence.

An uneasy pact, a truce without words.
Shame is their core, Shame is their whore

Because she knows they will sell her out
Giving away her hidden, dark black world

A friendship borne of humiliating guilt,
Skeletons hiding together, apart.

With bitter understanding, she kisses Fear and Silence goodbye
as the waves of Judgment nip and bite.

Shame inhales a shaky breath
Naked and lonely

Speaking her truth,
she is alone in the shimmering light.

Scratching 'til You Bleed

I'M NOT SURE HOW OR WHY I started writing nonfiction essays. Well, I take that back. I started out in Journalism, so crafting a story about real-life happenings became ingrained in my mind starting in college and when I sold my first stories.

My first two books are primarily satirical humor, essays based on relationships between men and women—a subject ripe for the funny. When it came to writing my third book, I just couldn't bring myself to write more humor. Humor comes naturally, sure, but there's another side to me that I felt compelled to share.

I had already started writing about dealing with the recent suicide of my ex. Grief and loss are big topics and deserving of an entire book, or ten, but I wasn't ready to write an entire book based on grief. I had more to write about—subjects that I'd never spoken about before, save to a few select people.

A fellow author-friend asked me to write a letter for his blog. A letter to someone I felt had wronged me in some way. It didn't take long for me to think about writing this piece: *A Letter to the Pedophile Next Door*. Well, I take that back. I thought about it for about six months—then I felt ready to write it. And I did.

What I didn't realize at the time—what was so seemingly obvious—was that this writer friend had given me permission to discuss an extraordinarily difficult topic. Permission that was there the whole time, but that I didn't see—couldn't see—because I was still that little girl entrenched in the shame of it all.

I even went so far as to ask writers I admire what they would do: tell a story if it can hurt people or keep it buried, doing what is accepted and "normal." I received opinions ranging from:

- It's a boring, downer subject. People only want to read happy stuff.
- If it will hurt of embarrass family or friends, you're better off not writing it.
- Go for it!

And yet, as I greeted my long-lost thoughts at the door, it felt right. I gave myself permission to write my story, from my perspective, with my rules. I let myself in.

Write something you'd never show your mother or father.

~ Lorrie Moore, Author

Many authors are unable to do that, and that's too bad, because it's a barrier to creativity. Ultimately, I did show my folks my book (my mom is an avid reader of anything and everything), and I value her input from a historical perspective, getting those pesky details right. But it's still my perception that counts.

I released my third book, *Broken Pieces: Essays Inspired by Life*, and the response has been nothing short of incredible. Award wins, nominations, bestseller status, and five-star reviews abound, which stuns me. I've also signed with a publisher who will create a print version in the next few months.

But what has been most gratifying, beyond all that, are the connections I've made with other adult survivors of childhood sexual abuse, with suicide-left-behind loved ones, with both men and women who suffered abusive relationships.

I also had to get over my own insecurities. Was I truly a "writer"? What would those who matter say about my work? Did I know enough about the craft of writing?

That too held me back, as it does many writers. But guess what? You won't know what you know and what you don't know 'til you sit down and write! What holds back most writers? *Insecurity*. Do we know enough about the craft? What if people don't like our work?

Let it all go. Go ahead, take a nice, deep breath and let all that junk free.

I experienced that for YEARS. And then I decided to do something about it. I took all those creative writing courses and what I learned in college and tossed them out the window. Instead, I wrote from my gut. I stopped worrying about others (and who are these invisible "others" anyway?), opened my veins, and bled (a la Hemingway's quote).

I laugh when people say writing nonfiction is easier than fiction. There is nothing easy about writing, period. And there shouldn't be. No matter what we write, no matter who we are, if writing is our thing, then own it—because when you put yourself out there, you'll feel vulnerable and scared. Just like you did when you were a kid.

And so what? Our vulnerabilities are what connect us and ultimately, what bonds us.

RECIPE

How can we miss what we never had?

I ALWAYS THOUGHT I could create something from nothing, filling a blank page with my darkest squiggles and lines, creating a sentence or paragraph to soothe, melting me into the pages.

Now I know I am far, far less.

And so much more.

My presence, all that is required to wander through his day— someone to bother for money or chores, someone whose name is "do this, do that," a faraway distance from the honeyed sweetness one savors on the tongue, mourning every swallow, the lost sugar of a fool.

You cast your hollow murmurs of love and wanting, floating them by me as if I won't notice all you're holding out, hoarding the missing ingredient, the bitter graininess I never developed a taste for.

That acerbic taste of pride mixed with withholding.

Forgive me, lover, for I have sinned.

I gave up faith in you and nothing tastes good anymore.

Pushing Through

DENYING THAT A BAD THING has happened is easy.

Then something happens: you remember. In chilling, graphic detail, you remember. And then time moves into a pile, no longer waiting, no...demanding you clean that mess up.

The bad thing takes your brain hostage, fills it with the detritus of denial, becomes dead leaves waiting for the deep scratch of the rake.

Survivors of any kind of trauma can have flashbacks. I'm no different. Flashes hit me of my abuser doing things to my small body and I push them away with the cold dissociation many victims of abuse know too well—a repeated loop of a movie we never wanted to see.

Dissociation becomes your friend when you've been abused. It's the black sheep sister of denial. Then along comes depression, the mysterious friend who appears out of nowhere, pulling us in with seductive promises of sleep, calm, and a clean place to rest.

I'll never forget how the depression and loneliness felt good and bad at the same time. Still does.

~ *Henry Rollins*

This quote resonates with me deeply because, as an adult survivor of childhood sexual abuse, I hit that wall of depression and anxiety in my thirties with a kind of unexpected welcoming fear. In all likelihood, I had depression and anxiety earlier—in my teens even—my parents trying to understand when I explained that I couldn't get a deep breath and the doctors could find nothing wrong. When my wrists swelled up painfully and the MRI showed nothing. When my headaches started. Headaches—an insidiously easy way to disassociate myself from life with pain and prescribed medication.

It's the perfect escape, isn't it? Valid disassociation.

When our family doctor suggested it was anxiety, we blew it off. I was a straight-A student, a fairly good kid, a gymnast and cheerleader. I was the model kid, as far as anyone knew. What did *he* know?

When in reality, I got high. A lot. I snorted whatever, and drank. I fooled around with random guys at parties, never going "all the way" because I was the good girl, ultimately ending up with the bad boy who loved me intensely, yet hated the good in me—that push and pull too hard to resist.

I tried so hard to have people think good thoughts about me, knowing in my heart that the good time I was searching for was a distraction, nothing more. Controlling that which is impossible, as many survivors do. Pushing hard to be the best made people focus on the perfect picture instead of looking for hairline cracks and loose pieces. Distraction all the way around.

From having to see my abuser every fucking day (he was my next door neighbor), who returned home to his family and job following a two-year sentence for molestation. From having to see his kids at my school, shooting me dirty looks, as if I were the filthy one.

Oppression, repression, depression.

I testified twice—once in the civil trial and again for the military. I remember what I wore that day the army officer picked me up, I remember my hand on the Bible, I remember sitting in that uncomfortable chair. I don't remember my words…I must have been so ashamed at what I had to say; apparently it was enough to put him away for a few years.

As an adult, I know logically that it wasn't my fault. I shouldn't have felt ashamed. But as a terrified kid, I slipped into that dissociative state, with a buzzing in my ear, people moving in

slow motion, all those eyes on me, talking about something some preteen shouldn't know about, let alone have to tell a room of strangers.

Twice.

Shame, fear, and denial became friends I never wanted and didn't like. Bad things happened and my entire family lived in guilt and denial. We still do to an extent. But we all moved on. I don't blame my folks.

I blame him. The dead pedophile.

So how is it that I didn't become a runaway or addicted to drugs, alcohol, sex, or lying in my bed waiting to die? I honestly don't know. I still have headaches, anxiety and depression. Events can trigger me. I cried for days reading about the girls in Ohio, rejoicing in the death of their abuser, yet knowing that nothing, and everything, changes.

People suggest I need to forgive my abuser, but to me that implies he had no control over his actions, that his mental illness prevented him from stopping his actions. I don't believe that. He knew right from wrong. He made a choice.

Survivors create survival mechanisms. Mine is pushing through. I push everything to the side, out of my line of vision, out of my mind and I focus relentlessly on my goal. Not sure what you'd call it, but who cares? I'm a fighter and that's enough.

I live each day happy to wake up each morning to my children's bright eyes and warm cheeks. If pushing through gives me more days with the family I've created, with my writing, with my loves—fine by me.

Call it what you want. I call it living.

I MISSED WHAT YOU SAID

I MISSED WHAT YOU SAID.
I can't hear you over the seething silence of my anger.

The loud crush of my resentment drowning all but the moving of your jaw, watching you chew your words as if masticating a large bit of grisly steak that refuses to disintegrate.

It would not be overstating how much I hate that you love me. I realize how awful that sounds but I see it for what it is: an excuse. Your words mean nothing when you scoff at my feelings with belittling condescension.

How much I despise your assumptions and self-importance. That anything you do carries so much more weight than anything I could possibly imagine, as you laugh in derision at most everything I say.

But you are in for a terrible surprise because I see who you are. The man who considers sex as affection. Who disrespects and devalues. Who doesn't appreciate the fleeting moments passing him by.

Love can exist without desire but is that what we want? To settle?

The moments are done, gone now. We had intensity, mellowed down to passion, filtered now with apathy. Not near enough to carry us through this life. At least, not for me.

It's over. It has been for a while.

I'm out of breath because words don't matter anymore.

PULL

Your silence is deafening
I pray you'll speak
Tell me what's in your soul
Tell me I haven't ruined it.

You shut me down
"No emo, tonight"
Not meaning to crush
This tender heart you cherish.

Breaching your trust
My mind plays its tricks
Detaching, roaming,
Searching for my anchor.

You command, I accept
Not without rancor
"I won't break," I insist,
As you bend me.

Moving forward
Looking back
Binding me to you
Owning my heart.

Pulling me close
Mesh across my skin
Separated by
My light in your dark.

Strong and independent,
Soft and willing,
You quiet the chaos
I travel your whim.

EVERY DAY SINCE OCTOBER

I've thought about you, my Dark Prince
Every day since October.
The fall you carried
Folded tightly into your heart.

Nobody has ever known the me I hide inside
The little girl alone in the middle of the heavy crowd
Looking to you for guiding love
Folding me into you.

All the times we haven't yet had
Living the way we've only desired
In lonely, hidden dreams that we
Folded into ourselves.

Entwining amber thoughts and burning bodies
My skin craving yours, minds rolling in possibility
Your light blending into my dark, your roiling sky
Folds into my glassy ocean.

I hear the beating of the waves you carry in your chest
That simple and that profound
This love that binds us
Folded into pieces inside love's soul.

Mated by this stunning universe that cannot contain us
Mystery tempered by edges of brokenness
That somehow meld together
Folding you into me.

It's not about me, it's not about you
This connection, larger than our words
Smaller than exploding cells combined
Folded into our hearts.

I've thought of you, My Dark Prince
Every day since October.
My fall you carry
Folded tightly in your hand.

BEFORE THE AFTER

IF YOU'VE EVER SURVIVED anything traumatic, you are changed. Traumatic experiences can be a part of everyone's life—it's all in the degree. Getting busted for smoking a cigarette or losing your bike may be the most traumatic thing you've ever been through as a kid—but to you, it's a big deal and could potentially be a turning point for you.

Someone who is sexually abused at any point, but particularly as a young child, will forever and always look at themselves as who they were before, and who they became after. We can't voice it, but we feel inside that something important that was there, that was waiting to be found, is now gone and we will always miss it.

There's no more purity once a molester has infected an innocent child with abuse. There's no antibiotic that can remove the bacterial invasion from what's left of their once-carefree life.

There's no more before the after.

It's something we hide inside the deepest pockets of our corduroy jumpers, used to holding things like twigs and gum. You don't walk up to someone and say, "Hi, I'm Rachel, and I've been sexually abused." It's not polite, it's not appropriate dinner conversation, and it makes people uncomfortable, these dark secrets.

It makes *us* uncomfortable. We dissociate—seeing ourselves as someone else, using humor

or anger

or drugs

or lovers

or alcohol

or food

or self-harm

or exercise

to cope

to deal with the after. The before is long gone, something we didn't mean to leave behind as we would a hat. A thing. Rather, our innocence is stolen from us, taken from us by men with big hands and guns, without permission. We are too young to understand, but we know it's hard and it's wrong and it makes us want to crawl out of our skin—it makes us no longer feel like children.

We watch our friends crying over their doll's broken leg and we laugh at their innocence—not because we want to make fun of them, but because we take joy in the fact that the doll's broken leg is the worst they've ever dealt with, and we pray for them that the trivial will continue to have meaning. Because we know.

Because we see the bigger picture, albeit in small, tiny slivers that don't fit together, because we know it's useless to try to repair something that cannot, will not, be fixed. We are no longer whole—we are bits of cells made up of dread, and fear, and shame. We speak in terms that separate us from ourselves because even now, all these many years later, we don't want to own what happened. We didn't engineer or control it, we didn't want this...this after-place that hurts more than the abuse.

That doesn't ever go away.

We quash the memories, put them in a drawer we lock with a key we wear around our neck, flashes that pull tight, choking us into remembering that which we can never run far away from, a home where we can't hide from ourselves, the place that should be but no longer is our sanctuary.

The after is a place none of us wants to be.

DEPRESSION

They fly past me
In the misty gray light
Sometimes I catch them,
And others I simply watch as grisly, chewed on bones dance by.

Flashes of white
Slashes of dark
Cut into my side
The greasy-haired man
Invades more than my dreams.

I fold the memories up
Into neat little pieces
Of origami eyes and hair and smiles.
Where do I put them?
Where do they go?

No matter how tiny I press them down
Slivers of horror unfold.
He's not here anymore…

Can a ghost of air and dust
hold me now?

This weight is heavy
Maybe I'll never get over this
Maybe I already have
Pulling me down in the misty gray
I drop the pieces, watching them fall

Some break, some don't.
Strong isn't as easy as you see
Falling slowly
Hiding, clawing for purchase
Fighting for this life

One small piece of me
Holding it tight just to let it go

ICARUS

Time winds its way around the sun
Carrying fears, tears, and loss
Love stretching from seconds to days to years
Striated patterns of memory across a lazy sky.

Time whispered to me
In whiskey-laced murmurs
"Come here, little girl,"
And I do.

Inside sleep, I can breathe
No fears, tears, or loss
Even the nightmares run
Because they know he's here now.

Takes a strong man who
Can scare away my terror,
In my deepest subconscious
I come when he calls.

He heals me with his voice
He calms me with his heart
Free from heavy burdens
With him, I come undone.

I fly up to the sun.

THE QUIET CHILD

AFTER EXPERIENCING SEXUAL ABUSE at the hands of my next door neighbor (an adult man, in the army, a father of five) when I was eleven years old—and subsequently testifying in both civil and military trials which helped convict him and court-martial him—I became the quiet child.

THE EXPLOSION

Always an introverted, serious kid, I withdrew further into my safe world of books and music in my room, rarely venturing out other than for school, meals or chores. Because if I did, I faced the glaring, accusatory stares of his wife and children—as if I were the one who committed such ghastly crimes.

This was the 70s, and though my parents carried tremendous guilt about what happened, therapy was something for my crazy Aunt Barbara who existed on cigarettes and Thorazine between her many botched suicide attempts.

I didn't need therapy. I was good. I was fine.

Except, as most survivors know, I wasn't. I drank, got high, partied—a lot—and while I surprisingly didn't sleep around, I was that straight-A, smart with a side of nerdy cheerleader to appeal to both jocks and geeks. In other words, I was never without a boyfriend or at the very least, a prom date.

THE AFTERMATH

It really wasn't until I had my first child (a daughter, now almost fifteen) in my mid-thirties that I sunk into a heavy, gray mix of depression laced with anxiety. Despite hiring a wonderfully sweet, qualified nanny, and knowing that my husband, a solid, good man, worked from home and could keep a keen eye on them both, leaving her to return to my sales job sent me into a loop of fear that made normal existence quite impossible.

Fortunately, I reached out to my fabulous doctor, my gynecologist, who asked if there was something in my past that would perhaps cause me to…well, freak out. After giving a brief description of my childhood experience, she hugged me tight and then handed me a prescription for Prozac and the name of a qualified shrink.

THE HELP

I'll always be grateful for her loving, gentle manner and for seeing in me what I was incapable of recognizing in myself: that I was suffering from anxiety, panic disorder, and depression. Even, and most especially, PTSD. I entered therapy and found it to be life changing (along with a different anti-depressant, indicated for both depression and anxiety that I still take daily).

Now, as a fifty-year-old mother of two children, who has written three books (one, the bestselling, award-winning *Broken Pieces*, deals with my experience—as well as date rape, love, and loss—in the form of essays and poetry), I learn more every day about the effects of that experience and that they are, indeed, quite real.

My family (sisters, parents), while supportive, cannot imagine what I experienced and we really don't discuss it openly. Growing up, I'd hear my parents talk about it in hushed tones, telling people that my experiences weren't as bad as some of the other girls...you see, because there was no penetration, the multiple times he did sexually molest me were considered to be "less damaging." Yeah, think about that.

Multiple studies show that ANY type of sexual abuse is traumatic for a child, be it visually, with words, or through inappropriate touching of any kind. But back then, we didn't have that type of understanding. When people tell you that "it happened, you're fine, move on," you, as a compliant child, do just that.

Well, you try. And usually, fail. As I did.

It took until I was in my late forties for me to give myself permission to write about these difficult experiences. Like many survivors, I found myself worried that people would think I was exploiting myself for profit, that they would consider my experiences as no big deal—bad luck maybe, nothing to make a fuss about—or even that my family and kids would reject my project as vanity.

THE REALITY

Fortunately, none of that happened. In fact, I've connected with so many survivors, both male and female, that I created a private, "secret" group on Facebook (up to 50 members now) that serves as support—not therapy—for any survivor of CSA who wants to participate. It's been so gratifying to learn that what I experience even now isn't unique.

I also created #SexAbuseChat on Twitter—every Tuesday, 6pm PST/9pm EST, co-hosted by survivor/author/certified therapist Bobbi Parish. We welcome anyone to join in—survivor, family, friends—to help others find a safe place to discuss their own experiences and the aftermath.

The incidence of childhood sexual abuse continues to grow. Sadly, multiple studies show that the majority of victims are still young girls (some say one in six, others say one in 10, with over 60% [some studies say 85%) of the perpetrators a *male that they know*).

According to the National Center For Victims of Crime:

- 1 in 5 girls and 1 in 20 boys is a victim of child sexual abuse;
- Self-report studies show that 20% of adult females and 5-10% of adult males recall a childhood sexual assault or sexual abuse incident;
- During a one-year period in the U.S., 16% of youth ages 14 to 17 had been sexually victimized;
- Over the course of their lifetime, 28% of U.S. youth ages 14 to 17 had been sexually victimized;
- Children are most vulnerable to CSA between the ages of 7 and 13.

More than anything, I'm honored to be a voice for survivors, for those people who for whatever reason are not able to discuss their experiences. I will never be normal, but that's okay because normal wouldn't have created the situations that allow me to survive, to thrive, and to hopefully, help others by being the quiet child no more.

* * *

BODY

STEAL A KISS

Writers are always alone, even in a room
bursting with noises of the familiar.

YOU DON'T GROW UP THINKING, "I'll be the child who will be sexually abused by a neighbor man when I'm eleven." It's not like my parents raised me to be afraid of strangers for no reason.

But he wasn't a stranger. He was the Pied Piper of neighbors— fun, big, he made all us little kids feel safe. Until he didn't.

Until that first time, when he told me he was going to "steal a kiss."

All I remember is the sour taste of ash when he kissed me, his tongue so big I gagged. He laughed, holding me down while he did it again, my desire to puke all over his giant black shoes greater than my desire to run, as if my small body knew to purge this disgusting invasion.

That stopped him. That time, anyway.

I read the term, "steal a kiss," in a blog post recently and I felt my entire body chill, tears welling up, the urge to gag so strong. I don't think I'd heard that term in forty years, but my body remembered. My mind knew.

Triggers—some people are regularly triggered by words or phrases like this. I'm not. Well, not usually. I don't live in fear of triggers, or avoid situations because something might set me off. Yet sometimes things like this happen and I fold in upon myself, crawling into a fetal position, numb to the world.

And I hate it. I'm not a victim. I'm a survivor. I wouldn't be writing this book or sharing my story if what happened hadn't happened, or talking about this body section at all—so I don't see it as a bad thing, just as a thing.

Writing is healing. Talking is healing, but it doesn't change the facts. Abuse happens.

Another blogger recently told me that *women who complain or whine about having been raped or molested need to shut up, because they have no idea how good they have it here in the Western United States. They're lucky they aren't raped or tortured daily like women are in other parts of the world. They need to be grateful to have higher education, food and homes. "Little things" like being sexually abused as children or raped in college come with the territory.* I wish I was making this up.

I wish I could say it's shocking to me that this kind of misogyny exists anymore, yet I can't. I hear it daily—and not only toward women.

Here's the deal with triggers—when they happen, we recognize them and then decide which course of action to take. I can't possibly know if a book or movie will contain a phrase or scene that could trigger me, but I also don't live in fear that something will, either.

Because I will recover. I've been through worse. I'm still here.

AFTERSHOCKS

MY BEAUTIFUL MAN, strong, sexy, musky, masculine. I take him in, he holds me to him. I'm enveloped, lost in where I want to be. Nothing was amiss. Nothing that I could feel, anyway. I know my way.

And then memory punches me with brutal force and I stop, I move, I float away.

"Baby?" he asks, and I barely hear him in the fog of the thick cloud surrounding me, memory drowning out his voice, no longer feeling his warm skin against mine.

He is my anchor, my protector, but even he cannot navigate his way over this jagged road. Not because he won't try, because he will. Not because I won't allow it, because I do.

It's because I don't know. I don't see it yet…the flashes of terror, swerving tendrils passing my periphery, target practice, a near-miss, a direct hit. My body a tight ball of numbness. Neither of us knows how to recognize it. Like children in a foreign land, we instinctively huddle together to solve a problem we haven't figured out yet.

I can't find my way.

I retreat into sleep without letting him hold me. It kills him, but he gives me that. Tears in the morning, holding the messy shame of the forty-year-old memory right there in my open hand for him to see. Flesh and hair, genitals and lips—the human body is pretty much the same for us all; it's only the experiences that change.

That change us.

He holds me now as I cry, apologizes for not seeing, for not knowing. It's okay—I didn't know either. "It's not your war to fight," I say.

I get lost sometimes.

I've traveled this road for many decades and I still don't know how to go. I am a wanderer, traversing mountains of time. There is no fault, only fault lines that tremor and quake, barring me, no warning.

Aftershocks.

I tremble as I calm, breathing restored, working my way back through time's icy fingers, realizing it will always be there, waiting in the shadows.

This battle I know.

I know my way.

WHISPERS

Most people run away from their pain.
Running from the shards, the scratches, the scars
That travel from their hearts to their brains.
Curling tendrils drawing them in,
pulling them into the darkness.

You didn't run. You gave me the pain I craved,
The sensations I didn't know I needed
That I always shied away from.
Brought to me with lightning stabs
Loud as deafening thunder in your quiet whispers.

I ran, I returned
To be free from your sorrow
My Dark Prince, hiding in your light
The safe place you carry,
waiting for me
Waiting for my own gift of bruising marks.

Marks I claim with pride
Just as you have claimed me as yours.
It isn't always what we see that hurts the most.

Pain isn't always unwelcome
How will I know how strong I am
if you don't take me there?

ERECTION

AS ONE OF THREE GIRLS with no brothers and a very private father, I had never seen a penis. This sounds silly and laughable now—I'm almost fifty and I've seen plenty. But at the age of eleven, I didn't know what that long, hard thing was in my neighbor's dad's swim shorts.

New neighbors had just moved in. A whole big passel of kids. The girl my age, M, invited me over to swim. Living in the suburbs of Sacramento in the oppressive summer heat, damn hot all the time, I jumped at the opportunity to spend a day in the cool water with my new neighbor friend. My mom, thrilled not to have me underfoot, gave permission.

I felt it in my bones, the moment I got there, a strange vibe in their home. Messy and full, yet vacantly cold. It registered weird to me, on some primal level I'd never felt before, that her dad would be home in the middle of the day, given that I rarely saw my own dad before dinnertime. Stranger still, the huge erection he had in his swim trunks while he played with us kids. I didn't know, of course, that the thing in his shorts was called an erection. I thought he was being silly by putting something in his pants.

I simply had no concept of it. Of course I had no concept of it! I didn't know what an erection was or what it was called, because that's normal for an eleven-year-old. This situation pushed me out of normal innocence, thrusting me into a surreal situation I couldn't name, let alone verbalize to anyone.

It's sad and embarrassing to think that I was that naïve, but I was. "What's in your dad's pants, M?" I asked her, my child's mind not understanding but unable to look away. It reminded me of a scary movie: I didn't want to look but the phenomenon was so odd, so weirdly compelling, I couldn't help it. I'd simply never seen a man with that "thing" before. Was there something physically wrong with him?

She blushed furiously. "Just ignore him," she replied, clearly embarrassed also.

I'd remember that response later, reviewing events in my mind, with the police. This clearly wasn't the first time M's father had embarrassed her. More than that, we found out later exactly why they had moved.

He got into the pool with us to give us "boat rides," pushing us along while he stood close to us. Pressing my small gymnast's body against his, feeling his hardness against my rear, I wiggled away. I'd swum with my dad, uncle, and grandpa and never felt anything like this. My skin prickled with the chill of heat, as if I'd done something wrong.

Uncomfortable, I instinctively placed more distance between him and me. I didn't know what was going on with M's daddy, and while I loved the icy water in the stifling heat, my mind raced with unanswered, confusing questions. I left quickly.

My body and my mind knew though, screaming at me, "Stay away!"

THE COPSE OF TREES

I'VE NO IDEA HOW IT STARTED, but the neighbor dad started giving all the neighborhood kids scooter rides. We'd line up ("no pushing or shoving") on the hot sidewalk and wait our turn while he drove each child around the neighborhood's empty lots, foundations waiting for homes to pop up like Pete Seeger's little boxes.

At the end of the street, if you make a left and head up the hill, there's a copse of big, old oak trees, waiting to be cut down to make room for more boxes, their old limbs keeping watch.

This is where he took me.

My hands on the handlebars, excitedly taking a turn steering while his hands roamed, knowing I couldn't let go or we'd crash.

I could feel his breath in my ear as we stopped. "Why are we stopping here?" I asked. "I want to go fast!" I laughed. My parents certainly were not daredevils, and riding on a scooter was a chance to feel the wind in my hair and do something I'd never normally get to. It was fun!

Until it wasn't.

Until he kissed me with his tongue. I pulled away quickly, knowing this is not how the adult men I knew so far in my short twelve-year-old life would ever behave. It was smelly, disgusting.

He pulled me to him; "Feel this?" he said and took my hand around to his sweaty back where he had a gun shoved in his pants. "You will let me kiss you. And you won't tell anyone or I'll use this on your family," he told me, holding my arm in his vise-like grip.

Terrified, I gave in. I didn't know what else to do. Here's a very large man, over six feet five, his heavy jean-clad thighs pushing down on my small body, with a gun. He continued with his hands, his mouth, his demands, and I began to cry. It didn't matter.

Finally, he released me.

I ran all the way home, crying. I didn't want to be on that bike with that man anymore. I couldn't tell anyone– I didn't want him to kill my family. The fear, inescapable, pervasive. My heart racing, my skin crawling with the anxiety of this inexplicable outside world.

I stayed inside as much as possible until my mom couldn't stand my cartwheels in the house anymore and shooed me out to the front yard where I had a huge expanse of grass to play, where I could do flip-flops all the way across the yard.

Where he could see me.

He would stare at me, watching my every movement. I'd slink back into the house, my skin chilling under his gaze, my stomach in my throat, choosing instead to stay in our small backyard where I could only do one flip-flop. His daughter M would ask me over and I'd say no. My mom didn't understand why. "M seems so nice!"

And she was. She was a quiet, shy girl, very sweet. But I knew her secret. I don't know if she knew mine, but I'm sure she guessed. I didn't talk with her anymore. I couldn't, my words pushed down into that secret, sweaty place I quickly learned to hide, the beginnings of the rooms I hid inside.

And so it goes, when fear becomes your daily companion.

The old, dark oak tree behind my house, watching, seeing all.

Letting Go

There is still, there is always, that blame/shame thing going on between who we were and who we are now. You're stronger now—you will win.

IF EVERYONE SEES THE GOOD GIRL, maybe they won't know my secret. That I was bad. That I was ruined. That I had been used, broken, torn apart.

Hiding inside my studies, the danger of tumbling madly backward and forward through the air, pushing myself harder and harder, despite broken arms and pulled muscles, to achieve that ribbon, that award, that grade that will show them that I am good. Holding tightly to the fragments of what I need to be the good girl.

I am still good.

I get a D in math. I fail my driver's test. Typical teenage failures, yet I am devastated.

It's all a facade. I'm a failure. I'm bad. My grip starts to fail.

A little thing, a baby step backward, we dust off and try again. But I didn't. I cowered, I hid, I stuttered in embarrassment that the tester was a jerk and that it wasn't my fault. But it was. I made a mistake. Everybody makes mistakes. I wasn't allowed to make mistakes. I had to be perfect.

We learn from mistakes. What did I learn from my abuse? Not to trust. That I was alone, truly alone. That nobody would really ever protect me but me. That words carry meaning, but actions mean more. I held tight to the belief that I was alone.

I wanted my words to mean something. I wanted my actions to mean more. I stayed up studying, I practiced gymnastics for hours and hours, fatigue wearing down my bones. I tried out for this team and that—a way to show them, the proverbial them, or was it me, that I was *fine*.

I'm not sure anyone really paid all that much attention, but like most young people, our world revolves around us. The quiet girl with her nose in a book, the shy cheerleader who ran away to tumble instead of talking to boys who then dismissed her as a snotty bitch, her only courage a gin and tonic at a party, a toke of weed to make her brave enough to flirt.

Pushing the boundaries of my quiet reserve, seeking to loosen that thin gloss before it hardened into a permanent mask I could someday never break. It wasn't enough, the veneer of perfection. Perfectionistic tendencies create anxiety, create depression, create control issues. Spiraling, spinning, like the backflips I would do.

I had to let go.

Ambition to become someone—someone beyond his victim— carries me even now. I am smart, I am strong, I am a survivor. I protect myself and speak for those who can't. I still catch myself now and then wanting to control things and people, but I stop. I breathe. I think. I unclench my fists.

And let go.

NORMAL

I'VE ALWAYS MAINTAINED that I've never tried to kill myself. Never even came close. Never had thoughts about it.

Well, I didn't *think* I had.

But in reviewing memories from that time, that horrible awful time when my neighbor molested me, I realized I *did* think about it. I *did* have thoughts about it.

I was eleven.

When people discuss childhood molestation, the words they most often associate with the victims are: shame, disgust, and fear. Toxic things, all.

As an eleven-year-old (when my neighbor started the abuse), I couldn't verbalize—out of fear, disgust, and shame—that I wanted it to stop. That I'd do anything to make it stop.

Even kill myself.

Have you ever tried to go about your day, say, watch a TV show, while shoving down the bilious fear that all is not right with the world? Hold your baby sister, rocking her to settle her and hoping that you'll settle too, while knowing that maybe this world is maybe just too much? That maybe, just maybe, the only way out is to permanently leave?

I can see, now that I'm older, that I did consider suicide as a way to end that fucked up hell. I even went so far as to check out the pill bottles in my parents' medicine cabinet. The confusingly long names fortunately created a deterrent—how would I know if what I'm taking would do the job?

Fear combined with helplessness is acid eating your soul.

The long-term effects of abuse—any kind of abuse—they know, actually changes the biology of the brain. Does this make us abnormal? Given that one in 10 children will be sexually abused before the age of eighteen, it would seem otherwise (YMCA data, 2013).

How awful to think that those of us who were abused are the normal ones. My god, that's staggering. It makes me cry for our children.

Eventually, maybe, I'll cry for me. First I have to deal with the fact that I considered suicide as an option when I never thought I had. That's a realization that slams into you. Hard. I haven't dealt with it, beyond talking about it here and with my therapist.

I don't feel that way anymore, but I do feel it's important to uncover those wrappings and find out what's hiding in there. That little girl is still inside of me.

MONSTER INSIDE HER BONES

She feels you moving inside her
Your tentacled fingers snapping at her veins
Flesh recoiling, rotting at your touch
This monster inside her bones.

She sees you watching
Your body burning desire
The child looks away, confused
This monster inside her bones.

She hears you talking
Speaking words she's never heard
Startled, spinning away
This monster inside her bones.

She tastes your giant, ashy tongue
Pushing and pulling at her soul
Hiding inside her dreams
This monster inside her bones.

She smells your evil sweat
Assaulting every cell
Running from herself
This monster inside her bones.

SLITHER

Trust comes easily
When you believe men to be good
Shame on me for believing
That I deserved shame.

Like an unsuspecting child —
Not afraid, no reason to be.
It was a party and
You were sweet.

Banal terms, later
"He seemed so nice…"
Even you believed
That I deserved it.

Locking me in a tiny room
Tearing at my clothes
Baring your teeth, biting and bruising
Holding down your prey.

No pain in the pain.
Shock chilling my arms
Yet hiding inside my memory
Fury building. No, not again.

I will not go back to that place
Where panic and anger pull at my throat
Numbing silence catching my screams
As terror scrapes

The woman breaks through:

You have no fucking right!

I claw and scratch
Fight and fly
Over, around, and under
Your slithering skin mottled with sticky blood.
The dripping red stopping you
Taking your monster back inside its cage
The cage I imagine
Only held you … 'til the next one.

DANDELIONS

She remembers the exact moment,
Her childhood disappeared
Gone like an unexpected breath
Expelled like any other
Nothing special
Not a wish
Or a blow
Of a birthday candle
Or the floaty, feathery threads of a dandelion
Carrying wishes of cinnamon candy or tiny orange kittens
Away into the careless breeze.

She remembers wanting a tabby
Striped with a rough bubblegum pink tongue
That would make her giggle as it licked her nose and
Purring her into a warm, soothing sleep.
Something normal, like any girl would have
Instead of the dark shameful secret
Of a large man's hands
And things she doesn't know the name of
Touching her in places only a kitten should be allowed.

Lying in her cold sheets
Alone with only her thoughts
Fear pushing at her sides
Despite the careful way she diligently pulled up and folded her
Heavy blue winter blanket
Around her sides at night
The way she did
Each night
Before allowing herself
To finally, fully,
Lay her body down.

She wonders about the little girl with the kitten
Is she happy in her ribbons and curls?
Does she think of me as I think of her, she wonders as she
checks again
As she always does
That the window is locked and bolted, just to make sure
Because you never know if he could somehow get in, she tells
her dollies
And they listen intently with their shiny button eyes because
they know
What men are capable of, because
They see.
They watch.
They know.
She would hold her kitten safe and warm
It would never be scared at night
Because it would know she was home
Always a tiny kitten, her innocent baby
She would protect it and keep it close under her watchful eye
And comforting hands
Never let it wander off or blow away
Like the feathery threads of a dandelion
Far away and gone.

I'M NOT SORRY

I DON'T FORGIVE MY ABUSER. Not because I'm angry or because I'm not healed (which is a process anyway). It's simple really—as a survivor, I'm in charge of my recovery, not you. Not her. Not him. I don't have to do what you tell me. Just because you tell me that in order to heal I have to forgive the man who invaded my body when I was eleven years old, I don't have to agree with you.

Besides, why must I take action for something that wasn't my fault to begin with? I've taken on enough already.

It's extremely personal, it's my business, and I flat-out reject the notion that in order to heal I have to forgive him. In fact, it's not anyone's business but my own whether I forgive anyone for anything! Yet, survivors are constantly asked if we forgive our abusers. Why?

Asking a survivor of something so invasive as sexual abuse of any kind (but particularly of something that happened to us as children), if we are able to grant grace to someone for something so egregious, unlawful, and horrific, something that filled us so deeply with confusion and anger and shame—I find to be almost as invasive. It again puts the onus on the victim of the crime to DO something, when we were not at fault to begin with.

There's also a pervasive religious dogma in our culture that is thrust upon us—an assumption that healing cannot begin or move to completion without forgiving the monster. This often comes from clergy or non-survivors, which reeks of hypocrisy, like a truck driver instructing a brain surgeon.

IT DOESN'T ALWAYS WORK

Survivors each walk their own path, and many will share their stories of recovery, which may or may not include forgiveness. One friend (a single mom) tells of being forced to continue to work in an office with the man who raped her because her bosses told her she'd be fired if she reported his crime. Not only that, but she was told to forgive him in front of her superiors as well as HR, so it would go on record that she would not be pressing charges.

After a failed suicide attempt, she quit her job, brought charges against both him and the company, and is now working as a freelance artist. She's not angry anymore, but also says she'll never forgive him or the company for the emotional damage.

DO IT ONLY FOR YOU

Another survivor friend (who is religious) shares that she forgave her abuser because it helps her get through the day. She didn't want to carry the guilt and shame anymore, so by forgiving him, she let all that go. Forgiving him helped her forgive herself, and that's the only reason she was able to get to that point.

In fact, part of her recovery is group therapy with recovering pedophiles. I have the ultimate respect for her for being open to that. That's not something I feel I could do.

OR DON'T DO IT AT ALL

Many therapists will tell you that forgiveness is not a required step to healing, despite what religious leaders will tell you. For me, religion has no place in my personal recovery. I am a spiritual person, but I rejected organized religion long ago. It doesn't mean I don't pray or believe in certain things—it also doesn't mean I don't believe in forgiveness as a general rule.

What I believe in for me, and for all survivors, is the right to follow our own paths, and not to be pressured by people who, despite good intentions, feel the need to tell us how we are supposed to heal.

Who are these people, total strangers, who feel the need to force us to take action for a crime we didn't commit?

There are bad people in this world who do bad things. I don't believe it's part of my journey to give them a pass, to tell them it's okay. In my particular case, my abuser is dead. That doesn't mean it's too late to forgive him and maybe, someday, I will. Maybe I already have.

If and when I do, you will be the last to know.

* * *

SOUL

Eight Years

I WALKED UP THAT HILL for eight long years. After.

Living next to my abuser and his family—the neighbor to the left—an army officer, a seemingly friendly man to the neighborhood kids—who abused me, and others, sexually.

My parents didn't move away. He did the crime—why should they have to be penalized? I understood their anger and defiance, yet I lay in my bed every night with dreamy thoughts of moving to a new town, a new school, a new neighborhood where people were nice and didn't glare at me every day, as if I were the criminal.

"It didn't just happen once, and she wasn't the only one. The other littler girls' abuse was much worse. She's fine."

That's how my folks talked about it in hushed tones to family and friends, who stopped talking when I entered a room. Discomfort, shame, embarrassment, and guilt became my companions in my home, at school, everywhere I went.

I've talked extensively, now as an adult, with my parents in uncomfortable, stilted conversations about their thoughts and reasoning of that decision. Of not moving away.

Of not putting me in therapy—it was the mid-70s. Nobody really knew or understood that therapy wasn't only for the mentally ill. I was fine.

Of minimizing it.

As a parent, I can't imagine the guilt they felt, along with denial and shame. Not much different than what I felt, really, without the accompaniment of the actual abuse to mess with their heads… yet imagining what happened to their little girl surely affecting them. I feel for them now, as a parent myself. I truly can't imagine it.

Most of my growth, mentally and physically as a teen, consisted of trying to achieve perfection. Straight As, varsity cheer and gymnastics, always doing the extra credit, zero period, and AP classes. Writing and writing and writing. My one and only D, in Geometry (which I still never use, thank you very much), crushed me. My folks didn't really care much about that one D—knowing how hard I had studied and all—but it hurt. It stung. I failed.

Maybe I wasn't fine.

I drank, I smoked weed, did the occasional line of coke at a party, made out with boys who always pushed for more. I didn't give up my virginity—that wouldn't have kept me "perfect"—until I turned eighteen. And only then with my long-term boyfriend.

People partied, a lot, in the late seventies, early eighties. I saw no reason to be different. It helped me fit in. It numbed that heavy burden I neatly tucked into a special hidden drawer every night. Some days I forgot to take it out. Eventually, I left it there, never forgetting, but shoving it all the way in the back; avoiding, pretending that weight of shame didn't exist.

Climbing that hill every day.

Eight years of hyper-vigilance is a long haul, made heavier with all I carried. Once I moved, I *moved*. Away for college, then away for a job, then 3,000 miles away for a promotion. It wasn't far enough.

Distance and time don't diminish, can't change, trauma. You don't wake up one day done with it. It haunts you, as a ghost glides through your soul, a chilling disturbance in the lonely quiet of even the warmest nights, because the dark desperation still comes.

I still climb that hill, though the terrain is different and the burden less. The emptiness where purity and innocence used to dwell, forever gone at age twelve, now replaced with a survivor, a strong woman who finally decided to stop running, to stop perfecting, to stop climbing.

To breathe.

Eclipse

I'm going to wake up yesterday
and know what I shouldn't have done.

I'll remember to sleep with the lights on, so nightmares plaguing me
won't stand a chance of
taunting with their
quiet, evil whispers,
confusing shadows with light.

Whispers that draw me in with tempting caresses of stinging desire,
masks of the long-forgotten.

Floating ever-present, windows darkened by fear and honesty,
eclipsed by the brightest sun.

Piercing eyes waiting
Vigilant even in my sleep
Watching, listening for the rustling steps
To wake me one more time.

I'm going to wake up yesterday
and know what I shouldn't have done.

CLAY

PAIN, NOT UNLIKE CLAY, stretches and molds us into someone we never knew existed. There's beauty in that. Beauty most people can't, don't want to, or are afraid to see. Every scar we carry, physical or emotional, is unique. Nobody's pain feels exactly the same because I can't experience what you have. I don't know why you cry in the night. I can't tell you why I won't allow anyone to hold me in my sleep.

I only need to know you more than I need to breathe.

I feel your dreams, I hear your desires, I see your pain, not because you're hurting but because you're here, calmly holding my shaking hand.

Earning my trust, slowly, intensely, you walk me through my pain, carrying me safely through the flames licking at my back to the safest home in the world...the solace of your soul.

I've suffered. I've forgotten as much as I still remember.

But I can no longer wait. I don't rest when I sleep because my dreams are stifled need—for the pain I control, the hurt that only you comprehend—stinging tendrils you gift me, knowing, under-standing, teaching.

Mold my pain, Lover. Make me yours.

.

The Other Side of Words

I COULDN'T DO IT. I couldn't tell him. The gravity pushing me down so that I became a micro-version of myself, voice tiny, movements small.

"You need to go. I can't do this anymore," I say in a rushed, pained whisper, pushing it out before I can breathe it back in, before it can beat me down anymore.

He hangs his head. It was coming. He knew it was coming. How could he not? We hadn't fucked in years, hadn't touched in months. My desire for him ceased the day he lost my faith.

Such a complicated swirl comes to down to this, a simple haiku of randomly plucked words. It's over. It has been. Echoes of what we had torture us, but those are only ghosts, memories that taunt us with promises of what we once had. Happy pictures don't capture the resentful sadness behind our eyes.

You convince me that I need you, but I'm better alone. I have been for so long now. If being alone means depending on myself, on my quiet determination, on peace and gratitude, then I'll be making my way now.

I've learned that this is not my place. I'm not really who you think I am. I need more than you can give. I asked, you denied. I needed, you laughed. I gave, you took.

It's not all you. I can't give you what you need anymore. I'm not an actor. I can't fall at your feet and eat your words as if they are the best I've ever tasted. I'm a writer and words matter. And maybe that is my elemental, as crucial to me as water. I accept that words aren't the same ethereal, beautiful creatures to you. You used words, discarding them meaninglessly, without thinking, whereas I thought they held meaning.

I found what you will never see: that my love resides on the other side of words.

FRAGMENTS

WHY AREN'T YOU HERE FOR ME?
    As I cry alone in the shadows between what I need and what
you give, broken shards emerge, cutting through my glittering fog
of lust.
    Even the sun and moon fighting for your sea-blue eyes aren't
enough to make you see.
    Maybe you do. I can never tell. You hold back, you pull me close,
your eyes raging as you enter me, an anger I cannot soothe, a space
I cannot fill.
    Though I try to be the woman you desire, I realize I never can.
Because I already am, and it's not enough.
    Enough for me, I tell myself, as I gather my things. You don't
deserve me.
    Feel this? This is my anger at what could have never been.
    At myself for believing you were enough for me.
    Knowing fully why you aren't here for me.
    Taking your language into my soul, feeling it separate from
sentences to words burning with flight, 'til all I have left are mean-
ingless letters pushing fire through my veins.
    Words can draw blood if you're very, very careful.

NO BIG DEAL

A DOOR SLAMS AND SHE JUMPS.

An unexpected knock on the door and she startles. Normal, yeah?

A horror movie comes on and she cowers—so does everyone, right?

Except she can't get those images out of her mind and she cries for days, hiding in her bed, afraid of the dark, the nightmares that inevitably shake her out of her tremulous sleep. What grown woman does that?

Her daughter had a male teacher for fifth grade and she cried every day as she dropped her baby off for school. What if? Dear god, what if?

"What happened was no big deal. It wasn't as bad as what happened to the other little girls. It could have been so much worse! She's fine."

Minimization. Denial. Ignorance.

Sweep it under the rug. Move on. Keep the past in the past.

Except it doesn't work that way. Years, decades, of hiding inside a shame that grows like moss, tinting her a shade darker, yet not obscuring her completely, no matter how hard she tries not to be seen, for others not to know.

Everyone has their own definition of sexual abuse. Is seeing an erection inappropriate or abusive? Is touching abusive? Is forced sexual contact abusive? She didn't know. And according to those around her, only penetration or oral sex was considered "real" abuse, and she didn't even know what these terms meant at age eleven anyway.

He touched her inappropriately, several times. He forced her to touch herself while he watched. She saw his private parts. He kissed her. He said dirty, disgusting things to her, words with guttural sounds she didn't understand at the time. There was more. So much more.

But it was no big deal.

Abuse worms its way into a little girl's fretful soul, her confused brain, her fearful heart. She can't unsee, unknow, unfeel. Abuse doesn't unhappen.

It festers inside as her worried days grow to years, as sweaty, eager boys touch her breasts, the wet between her legs, shame building as she remembers his huge, wandering hands and his enormous tongue, and she cries because she enjoys it now, because there is something wrong with her, because it must be wrong. Arousal feels like shame, so she must be broken.

Nobody to talk to.

Alone in her guilt and confusion, she numbs her body with drugs and drink, not feeling the desire, only the rage of the confused, a fragmented idea of the person she thinks she's supposed to be. She finally gives herself to a boy with chocolate brown eyes, gentle and sweet, a caring boy who loves her. And then she leaves him.

No big deal.

And so it goes. Another boy, another heart, a life built on rage, shame, and confusion hidden deep inside her smiling veneer of success and ambition, layered with her fear of...what? Being found out?

She wasn't the only little girl to ever have been abused. So what? She's just one of the many. Nobody to listen, nobody to hear.

No big deal.

DREAMING

AGAIN, I FALL.
But I can't anymore. The pain intruding, surrounding me in that
fleeting moment where the swift air stops so abruptly I cannot breathe...
Leaning into the words you weave softly, so softly.
Frightened I'll miss the chance that never was.
Afraid I already have.

Sacrificing hope, I wear your love inside, pushed down deeply
into that quiet space no man can see...
Because he doesn't look.
You push me. You pull back. You want me, you don't.
If you crave my heart, then own it.
Are you man enough to try?
It's time for you to fall.

NIGHT

IT'S WHAT WE NOTICE after the fact that carries meaning, in the calm of the glowing moon.

My senses engaged, only you in my sight.

Your scent on my tongue.

Your words embedded in my heart.

Later, I'll remember your head on my breast, a tender moment of quiet inside the blur. Your seed inside me, staking your claim. Days later, months and years, I still carry you, cells merging souls.

Time replacing hope.

It's only in the quiet spaces between our stars that I feel you now.

One night burning inside us, a memory we return to, an infinite weaving of thought and fiery touch.

What is this inexplicable distance we cross in our dreams?

It is those moments of dark silence that give us our truth. There's no denying a love that has nothing to prove. It exists on its own.

Or passes us by.

CRACKS

HE SPEAKS TO ME in that low growl, his hazy shade of winter voice whispering softly, "Mine."

A simple word, really, yet one that carries more weight than anything I've ever held. I love being loved by him.

I imagine my life without him, hearing the ping of an empty hallway I crawl through, calling his name, wandering off the edge of my world.

He hears me when I'm so filled with the silence of sadness I can't speak, through tears so salty and full of anger I'm in danger of cracking, stroking my skin with calm, slender fingers.

Wandering his way back to me, "What's wrong, Doll Eyes?" he asks, and I am sure at that moment that nothing could ever be wrong again.

FIGHT

I fight this feeling
That I'm not good enough
Or pretty enough
Or smart enough

Your breath on my neck
Waking me with need
Wearing your desire
Like ink on your chest

"Please don't be upset
I didn't mean to do it
I didn't mean to forget"
Crying that I have failed you

You hold me close
Speaking in calming waves
"You haven't failed me
I learn you from your imperfections"

I don't understand
How is it possible?
I take what I deserve
Paying with my tears

You wipe them away
Holding the world
Up and away
Soothing my heart.

"Do you promise to trust me?"
"Do you promise to love me?"
That's all I ever wanted, I say
As you circle my soul.

FORGIVEN

Will she be forgiven?
Will light ever throw its gaze on her? Searching for safety in
dark silhouettes that cling to shadows, filling up spaces with
lust, dusty echoes of something akin to love…

They'll say she's selfish.
They'll say she's a silly woman acting like a girl.
And she'll agree.
And decide that she won't wait anymore.
She's a fool to leave the arms of one man into another.
She's a fool not to.
The truth lies, when it hurts and festers inside a soul that died
long ago.
The truth awakens her with a luminous kiss and she walks
away, melting into his warm fire.

There is more to life than forgiveness wrapped in sand and guilt
There is more to surrendering what's no longer there.
Taking her carefully to the edge, showing her the glimmer of
what will be

Taking her soul in his hands, building a trust he keeps cocooned in his heart.
Forgiveness is not what she seeks in broken panes and shattered frames
Forgiveness is clouds when she's looking for sun.
Her life, now tatters, when she glances sideways at the periphery
Her life, beyond grace, shredded by hurt and shame
She moves beyond flattened petals pressed in her past, placed safely on her shelf
She moves beyond, looking beyond, past, and in, moving into her own light…
She moves.

RELEASE

SHE BATS HIS LOVE ABOUT, as a cat with a mouse. It's not like she intentionally ever wanted to hurt him. She loved him, with pure feeling unencumbered by the red-flagged reality.

But he feels her moving out of reach, her body no longer pliant in his hands, no longer rising in climax to his touch. His fear of losing her taking a backseat to upsetting her.

The truth of it is, where there once was passion, there now is a tentative friendship, an almost easy kind of love one takes for granted—like thinking you have gas in your car, until you get in and realize that the tank is empty.

Nowhere to go.

She slips on her words, unsure how to proceed. So she stays out of reach, seeking, exploring, hoping for the more that isn't and maybe never was. He follows behind, waiting, waiting, waiting.

A decision awaits them both—she admits she's wrong, misunderstanding what they were with where they are, who they've become. Directionless, he searches desperately for a guide, a route to follow his woman to understanding.

Lost in her waiting, lost in his consternation, they watch the unfolding until all that is left are the scraps of a map to isolation... and release.

CLIMB

It's beautiful, this hill we climb
To the quiet, most private silence of our souls.
Where I have access to your dark places.
Where you need me.
Where I belong.
Where you live.

Like explorers in the night,
Who touch and lick and suck
Uncovering the sharp quivers that stab us
With love, with desire,
Heated flames
Of craven desire.

You hurt me with a single word,
You love me with your many.
Moving inside you, demons fight for flight.
You are my book, holding me in your hands.
You read me.
You see my story.

I calm your dragon,
I bring out your beast
Walking along the edge of us
I trace my fingers along your hot skin
Flaming our hearts,
Calming our minds.

We climb.

Books

HIS DEEP BASS TIMBRES vibrate against her cheek as he reads to her. She stretches, luxuriating in the feeling of his smooth, warm, dark skin against her pale and freckled, chilled except in the places where his body burns into her memory. Lying next to this beautiful man, spent and exhausted, he told her from the beginning that he wanted to read her to sleep, a gift he'd never given another.

That was it. She was *gone*.

The words don't really matter. It's his cinnamon voice that soothes her, his robust, thrumming heartbeat as night falls around them, his solid arms holding her in that loose but close way he has, slow breaths relaxing her, protecting her in his musky chocolate space.

Her mind wanders as he reads her favorite book, one she's read so many times she knows the story forward and backward. But she doesn't know it with him. Occasionally, a word pops out, scrolling like a banner in neon-green bubble letters across her mind, spoken in his slow cadence instead of her usual rushing by. It makes her wonder how much else she has missed—not only in reading but also in life, hurrying through it on her own.

Seeing things through his calm, Zen voice opens her eyes and scares her a bit. What else has she missed? And as always, his voice brings her back. He checks on her with his little arm squeezes and eye checks—this man who has loved her from almost Day One. How is this possible?

His mouth moves and she's mesmerized. She hears his voice, his heart, his skin, his long dark hair brushing her shoulders, her senses saturated with him to the point that she finally lets go, relaxing further. Her past has made her constantly vigilant, even in sleep. He's keeping watch. It's okay. It's finally okay.

She watches him beneath dark lashes, lost to the lazy song of his voice coupled with his full pink lips that she loves to bite for some primal reason, his amazingly talented tongue that makes her blush whenever she thinks about the way he makes her writhe and beg, and before she realizes it, a tiny moan escapes from the back of her throat.

Setting the book aside (he only reads "real" books to her), he pulls her closer.

"What is it, Little One?" he asks with a sly one-sided smile as he traces her lips with his finger, the way he does, always playing with her lips in some way or another that makes her feel like a kitten held by the scruff.

Her pale skin turning a deeper shade of scarlet, she drops her head. Too many images and words are running through her mind for her to make sense of it all. It's not only the incredibly physical connection they have. It's the deeply emotional way they've had since the start, the psychological bond, how they talk without talking. It's words. It's no words. It's all the silly love songs and the metaphysical and the poets and the movies and the romantics and how can it all possibly be them right there in that room and all be real? And it is.

It is.

And without another word, he pulls her even closer and holds her. He knows. He quiets her busy, overthinking mind, soothing her tangential soul, absorbing her fears of all that eats at her from the outside, from her past, from her now, removing it all with his slow, magical touch.

He is her lover, her healer, the one she found, the one who accepted her, who loves her damaged heart and works every day to sew her back together.

With words. Without words. The way he knows she will understand. With books. With touch. With love. With his heartbeat. With his heart. With his truth. With her truth. With breathing.

With him.

*   *   *

AFTERWORD

by Bennet Pomerantz

About two years ago, I had a show on Blog Talk Radio called *Anything Goes*. Rachel was a guest a few times, and we struck up a friendship. I loved her two satirical books, especially *A Walk in the Snark*, so Rachel invited me to write the foreword to her then-new book, *Broken Pieces*.

Rachel sent me an advance reading copy (we in publishing call them ARCs) of *Broken Pieces*, and I immediately saw that this project was a departure from her normal humorous style. It overwhelmed me. She wrote a powerful book. I expected another humorous essay book, but instead she wrote a collection of prose and poetry that amazed me.

In many ways, reading it felt like peeling an onion and trying not to cry. I kept yelling at the text on my computer screen, "This is damn f — — — good!"

At the same time she released *Broken Pieces*, I was planning a companion show to *Anything Goes*, called *Let's Talk*. I asked Rachel to be my co-host and she agreed. The show would not be as good as it is without Rachel's input and talent.

Since the release of highly-awarded and praised *Broken Pieces*, Rachel has started working for the *Huffington Post* as a columnist. Rachel never has a swelled head about her successes; she is still the same great lady I knew two years ago. She has an inner strength to survive—I can understand the pain she has felt by reading her words. She is one of the strongest women I know, as well as one of the bravest.

This book is a Herculean effort of emotions that I can only limitedly understand. She has my heart and my deep friendship.

Bennet Pomerantz
Host, *Anything Goes Talk Radio*
Co-host, *Let's Talk* and the *Legal Show* –
Blog Talk Radio
Columnist, "A Piece of my Mind" –
Night Owl Magazine

RESOURCE SECTION FOR
BROKEN PLACES

CRISIS RESOURCES

National Suicide Prevention Lifeline 1.800.273.8255 (They also have a
crisis chat feature from 2pm to 2am at: Suicidepreventionlifeline.
org)
Rape, Incest, Abuse National Network (RAINN) 1.800.656.HOPE
(They also have a crisis chat feature available 24 hours a day
on their website: RAINN.org)
Crisis Link Text Hotline (Twenty-four hour crisis help by text mes-
sage: CrisisLink.org/crisislinks-text-hotline)

BOOKS

Bass, E. and L. Davis (2008) The Courage to Heal: A Guide for
Women Survivors of Child Sexual Abuse. New York: NY.
Morrow Williams Paperbacks
Davis, L. (1991) Allies in Healing: When the Person You Love was
Sexually Abused as a Child. New York: NY. William Morrow
Paperbacks
Gil, E. (1988) Outgrowing The Pain: A Book for and About Adults
Abused as Children. New York: NY. Dell
Lew, M. (2004) Victims No Longer: The Classic Guide for Men
Recovering From Childhood Sexual Abuse. New York: NY.
Harper Perennial
Maltz, W. (2012) The Sexual Healing Journey: A Guide for Survivors
of Sexual Abuse. New York, NY: William Morrow Paperbacks

WEBSITES

Adult Survivors of Child Abuse—Ascasupport.org (Resources,
    support and information for Survivors of all forms of child
    abuse)
Fort Refuge: Abuse Survivors Community—FortRefuge.Com (An
    online support community for Survivors of childhood abuse,
    domestic violence and sexual assault. They have community
    forums and chat features)
The #NoMoreShame Project—NoMoreShameProject.Com
    (Information, Resources, Frequently Asked Questions for
    Survivors as well as publication of Survivor stories)
Rape, Abuse, Incest National Network—RAINN.org (Resources,
    Information and Crisis Help for Survivors)
Survivors of Incest Anonymous—Siawso.org (A 12 Step recovery
    group for Survivors of Incest, online resources and in person
    meetings)
Twitter Chat (Tuesday evenings at 6pm PST for Survivors of
    Childhood Sexual Abuse. Facilitated by Bobbi Parish and
    Rachel Thompson. Use the hashtag #SexAbuseChat to
    participate)
Google Hangout (Wednesday evenings at 6pm PST for Survivors
    of Childhood Sexual Abuse. Facilitated by Bobbi Parish and
    Athena Moberg. Live-streamed to The #NoMoreShame Project
    YouTube Channel)

* * *

ENJOY A SAMPLE OF
RACHEL'S FIRST *BROKEN* BOOK:

BROKEN PIECES

Rachel Thompson

PRINT ISBN: 978-1-62015-160-0

EPUB ISBN: 978-1-62015-256-0

CAGED

The right answer is to turn and walk away. But his arms are so strong and his words caress her soul. In his heat she abandons her resolve.

She's unsure how it started, moving from found to lost. One day she watches birds fly on apathetic wings, the next he stands behind her—his hands inside her heart.

He damages her new home, where she now lays her head, the place where guilt and lust meet.

But she cannot leave. His eyes hold her captive.

"You are mine," he tells her. "I own you now." She doesn't disagree.

Her breath quickens, her skin burns from the real and imagined hold he has on her. He whispers promises of life together, as long as all the pieces of her are his.

Pieces of her—
all he needs.

China Doll

I felt the storm break my heart.

Maybe I knew he had taken his life before I got the call; perhaps even before he left, his words a warning I didn't know to catch.

I can admit that now.

Before he died, when we spoke a storm brewed in his words. He had lost so many people—some he hated, some he loved. But still. So many deaths. Drinking ruined him; alcohol killed his marriage, twisted his relationship with his young son into sadness. He only told me bits and pieces. His language, sparse, as if he had created his own. I gleaned as much as I could from every conversation, trying to understand unspoken words, held breaths.

If only I had read between his lines.

If I closed my eyes, could I have touched his words?

"*SEE WHO I AM NOW!*" He angrily shouted, though his rage was couched between desire and love.

"I'm not that man anymore who would hurt you. You're my china doll, baby."

He carried me for twenty years, freezing me in time; taking me out, looking at me, before putting me back on his shelf. Who he thought I was. Not realizing I would grow and change, becoming a different person. A stronger person. A doll who didn't break quite so easily.

The mind warps what time can't forget. But I will never forget.

And I am not his doll. I am not fragile.

Then again, I'm not the one who broke.

LIGHT

Allow me to drape my limbs over you; my secret murmurs soothing fears that keep you awake as the rays of the day fade on borrowed rest.

Grasping your hand to keep you from losing your way back to me, you meet my eyes with a rush of desire that slams me in a hard, brilliant flash.

Do you hear me? I whisper along your skin, cooled by the night air. Crossing this wide river to you, I pray you'll reach for me as I pass by, drowning in your depths.

You, my only salvation.

Will you save me?

Waiting for the sun, I barely breathe so as not to wake you, unable to turn away from the glare of what we've wrought.

I bathe in our entangled gleam, where love lives inside the knowledge that tomorrow fades again.

Illumination only lasts until darkness decides to fall.

BIRD

He found me, waiting and bruised, pushing his way so deeply inside me; I never thought he'd find his way out.
But he surprised us both, shoving me aside as quickly as he'd come.
Using, abusing, he feared his inner darkness would disrupt our carefully structured nest.
Scared our pleasure would eat at his soul.
Too afraid to give room, or care, or thought, he left me as he found me, waiting and bruised, but now also willing and broken.
I shakily tend my wounds, mystified if I had flown, or fallen.

AND THEN I LET HIM GO

It hits me at the strangest times.

The fact that someone who was a part of my life is gone. *Here today, gone tomorrow.* A concept so hard to grasp when it happens to —

To whom? He's the one who took his own life. Nothing happened to me, his ex-love from many years ago.

We spoke earlier that day. The day he decided would be his last.

We never will again. Impossible.

But he visits me, in my dreams, conjured by my disbelieving subconscious.

Or is he conjured by my heart?

I wake up from the dreams confused and—somehow—relieved. In some, he tells me he's OK. In others he doesn't speak, but he shows me he's fine.

But there's still too much I don't know or understand about the man he became—this man I once shared my heart and body with. So I go about my days now, my full life bursting with my own family, and when he visits me in my dreams, I let him in.

And then I let him go.

ROOMS

Women have rooms inside of us men cannot fathom.

It's where we store the depths of the hurt we've been dealt.

Where we store the deep love we never want to lose.

Where we've tucked away all those cutting comments through the years, when we couldn't react because we had company. The place where we shoved the painful words down, swallowed the reactions and put them in the corner; pushing it all back down when it threatened to rise up,; afraid the tentative piece of string might snap and all the hurtful words he sent your way will tumble back out and hit him so hard he won't comprehend the language you're speaking is his own.

We fold our stories inside ourselves.

We unwrap them when nobody is looking.

We carry former lovers, long lost, inside our limbs. We feel their caresses, remember exactly how their tongues entwined with ours as our bodies melted, their eyes on ours as they entered us; even our cells remember the exquisite burn.

A woman never forgets, though she may learn to love another. We wrap those memories away for safekeeping, even when those lovers hurt and brutalize, our hearts break and we cry forever tears. We have a room for that pain, a special key we hide to lock it away.

Women grow, our hearts accommodating all the players in our lives.

We explore our rooms often, sometimes inadvertently. Our hearts won't allow us to ignore our secret places for long. Try as we might to suppress our desires, our unknown thoughts and fears will rise to guide us to different places, new rooms we never knew existed but were within us the whole time.

Embrace. Hold tight while you dance. Jump.

Our rooms are buried so deeply, many times we don't listen or can't hear. We fall, search, drift, let go. We hold our breath, worry what others will think, lose ourselves.

Don't.

Women have rooms inside us.

Breathe.

*   *   *

ABOUT THE AUTHOR

Rachel Thompson is the author of the multi-award-winning *Broken Pieces*, as well as two humor books, *A Walk In the Snark* and *Mancode: Exposed.* Rachel is published and represented by Booktrope.

She owns BadRedhead Media, creating effective social media and book marketing campaigns for authors. For affordable group sessions check out Author Social Media Boot Camp, monthly sessions to help all authors! Her articles appear regularly in *The Huffington Post, The San Francisco Book Review* (BadRedhead Says…), *12Most. com, bitrebels.com, BookPromotion.com,* and *Self-Publishers Monthly.*

Rachel is the creator and founder of the Twitter blog memes #MondayBlogs and #SexAbuseChat, and an advocate for sexual abuse survivors. She hates walks in the rain, running out of coffee, and coconut. She lives in California with her family.

AUTHOR CONTACT INFORMATION

Author Site: rachelintheoc.com
BadRedhead Media Site: badredheadmedia.com
Twitter: @RachelintheOC
Twitter (Business): @BadRedheadMedia
Facebook: https://www.facebook.com/AuthorRachelThompson
Facebook (Business): https://www.facebook.com/
BadRedheadMedia
Google+: https://plus.google.com/+RachelThompson/
Pinterest: http://www.pinterest.com/rachelintheoc/
LinkedIn: http://www.linkedin.com/pub/rachel-thompson/24/784/b95
Goodreads: http://www.goodreads.com/author/show/4619475.
Rachel_Thompson
Author Newsletter: http://eepurl.com/j9oaH
BadRedhead Media Newsletter: http://eepurl.com/koN8r

ALSO BY RACHEL THOMPSON

Broken Pieces (Memoir / Essay) Vastly different in tone from her previous essay collections A Walk In The Snark and The Mancode: Exposed, BROKEN PIECES is an award-winning collection of pieces inspired by one woman's life: love, loss, abuse, trust, grief, and ultimately, love again.

The Mancode: Exposed (Humor) Looking for a humorous take on family relationships, or love and romance? Look no further! Thompson deconstructs relationships with a keen, satirical eye in this humorous, #1 best selling essay collection.

A Walk in the Snark (Humor) It's not all humor, but it is all real. Humor and real life, with a little satire thrown in. Can you handle the snark?

MORE GREAT READS
FROM BOOKTROPE

Write for the Fight by **Tess Hardwick and Tracey M. Hansen** (Memoir) Heartwarming, funny and thought-provoking, Write for the Fight reveals the personal memories, fears and dreams of 13 writers as they reflect on defining moments of the past and dream of possibilities for the future.

American Goulash by **Stephanie Yuhas** (Memoir / Humor) A story about a nerd girl jousting with her Transylvanian family on the battlefields of suburban New Jersey for a chance to grow up authentically awkward and live a so-called normal American life.

Real Chick Lit for Real Chicks by **Meredith Schorr** (Ebook Collection) This boxed set brings together three favorites from best-selling chick lit author Meredith Schorr. Blogger Girl follows Kim Long, a book blogger asked to review the debut novel of her high school nemesis. In A State of Jane, "good girl" Jane Frank is looking for love, but when all of her dates flake out on her, she decides to turn the tables. In Just Friends With Benefits, Stephanie Cohen is determined to turn the one who got away into "the one." The stories are humorous, heartfelt, and definitely real.

Discover more books and learn about our
new approach to publishing at **www.booktrope.com**.

.

Made in the USA
San Bernardino, CA
22 January 2015